January

Months of the Year

by Mari Kesselring
Illustrated by Paige Billin-Frye

Content Consultant:
Susan Kesselring, MA
Literacy Educator and Preschool Director

magic wagon

visit us at www.abdopublishing.com

Published by Magic Wagon, a division of the ABDO Group, 8000 West 78th Street, Edina, Minnesota 55439. Copyright © 2010 by Abdo Consulting Group, Inc. International copyrights reserved in all countries. All rights reserved. No part of this book may be reproduced in any form without written permission from the publisher.

Looking Glass Library™ is a trademark and logo of Magic Wagon.

Printed in the United States.

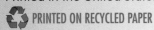 PRINTED ON RECYCLED PAPER

Text by Mari Kesselring
Illustrations by Paige Billin-Frye
Edited by Patricia Stockland
Interior layout and design by Emily Love
Cover design by Emily Love

Library of Congress Cataloging-in-Publication Data
Kesselring, Mari.
 January / by Mari Kesselring ; illustrated by Paige Billin-Frye ; content consultant, Susan Kesselring.
   p. cm. — (Months of the year)
 ISBN 978-1-60270-628-6
 1. January—Juvenile literature. 2. Calendar—Juvenile literature. I. Billin-Frye, Paige, ill. II. Kesselring, Susan. III. Title.
 CE13.K473 2010
 398'.33—dc22
                          2008050691

Do you know the 12
months of the year?
Are you ready to learn?
Then let's give a cheer!

January is the first month
of the year!
Coats, hats, and gloves
make good winter gear.

January is a long month
with 31 days.

That's plenty of time
to get out and play!

The first day of January
is New Year's Day.
We start a new year
with a hip hip hooray!

In January, people make
goals for fun!
These plans are called
New Year's resolutions.

In this first month,
some places get chilly.
We can play in the snow,
and we can act silly!

14

Let's build snowmen and forts,

skate, ski, and sled.

And when we are done,

we can climb into warm beds.

Or we might eat something warm
for our cold, hungry tummies,
like soup and hot cocoa.
Now won't that be yummy?

The third Monday is a day
for our friend Dr. King.
We learn about his lessons.
"Let freedom ring!"

The Chinese New Year is
during this time of year.
See the dragon in the parade?
It's nothing to fear!

January is over now.

But don't feel blue!

February is the next month.

There's a lot more to do!

Celebrate the New Year!

Have a party with some friends on New Year's Day! Play games together. Start the New Year off with a lot of fun.

Learn about Martin Luther King Jr.

January is a great month to learn about Martin Luther King Jr. He was a leader who helped many people. Ask a parent or your teacher to choose some books you can read about him.

Words to Know

February—the second month of the year. It comes after January.
freedom—being able to act or speak without being held back.
parade—when a group of people march down a street to celebrate a special day or event.

Web Sites

To learn more about January, visit ABDO Group online at **www.abdopublishing.com**. Web sites about January are featured on our Book Links page. These links are routinely monitored and updated to provide the most current information available.

DATE DUE

AUG 2 0			

GAYLORD   PRINTED IN U.S.A.